Learn How To Do Hand Sewing Stitches

Plus 20 Projects To Practice Your Skills

Sarah J Doyle

DEDICATION

This book is dedicated to those who would like to learn the fine art of hand sewing, and for those who want to teach children how to sew.

Mae,

Mimi is proud of your work at sewing. Since I cannot always be around to assist you when you hand sew, I wanted to bless you with this book that can help you and your sister with sewing.

Love,
Mimi
11/2023

CONTENTS

1	Introduction	1
2	Running Stitch	4
3	Back Stitch	5
4	Dust Cloth	6
5	Stuffed Tie Snake	7
6	Fish Bean Bag	8
7	Marshmallow Pillow	10
8	Overcast Stitch	12
9	Elephant Bookmark	13
10	Butterfly Pincushion	16
11	French Knot	19
12	Heart Bookmark	20
13	Blanket Stitch	23
14	Coin Purse	24
15	Denim Pocket Key Ring	26
16	Butterfly Applique	27
17	Baby Blocks	29
18	Hemming Stitches	31
19	Slant Hemming Stitch	32
20	Slipstitch Hemming Stitch	33
21	Vertical Hemming Stitch	34
22	Blind Hem Stitch	35

23   Make Your Own Reusable Heating Pad   36

24   How To Darn A Hole In A Sock   39

25   Cross Stitch   42

26   E-Z Sew Sewing Cards   43

27   Thread Hanger   48

28   Resources   49

29   About The Author   51

1 INTRODUCTION

Hand sewing is a very popular hobby and is easy to learn. Whether you're an adult wanting to learn the art of hand sewing or someone who is teaching a child to sew, the instructions, diagrams and assorted projects in this book can be used for people of all ages, with some projects designed for 3-5 year old children.

First, we want to show you a couple samples of hand sewing needles that we recommend.

The first example of <u>16 Embroidery hand sewing needles</u> are different lengths, sizes 3-9 that you can use for any of the projects included in this book. The second sample, <u>6 Chenille hand sewing needles</u> we recommend for children ages 8-12 because of the larger "eye", making them easier for children to thread, and being a thicker needle they will be easier for children to hold for hand sewing.

To begin our hand sewing instructions, we'll show you how to thread a needle so you'll be ready to start sewing. Next we'll give you illustrations of basic hand sewing stitches and instructions on how to make the stitches as well as project ideas using each of the particular stitches.

Cut a length of thread from the spool that measures approximately 20" – 30". The maximum length I'd recommend is 30", which would give you 15" of length after making the knot at the bottom of both ends (B).

Figure A

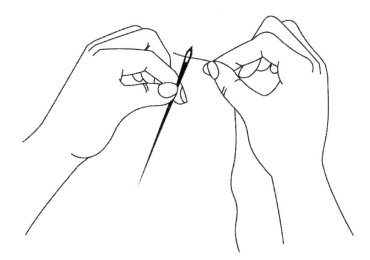

(A)   Insert one end of the thread through the eye of the needle.

Figure B

Double Strand Knot

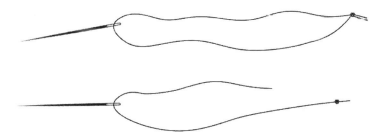

Single Strand Knot

(B)   Make a double strand knot by bringing the ends of the thread together
       and tying them into a knot as close to the ends as possible

(C)   You're now ready to begin sewing.

2 RUNNING STITCH

It's always a good idea to do some practice stitching before you start the "real" project. Draw out a couple 8" – 10" lines on small pieces of firm fabric, such as denim or cotton duck cloth, then practice the following running straight stitch a few times.

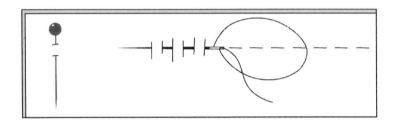

The first and most important stitch you'll use (and practice first) is the RUNNING STITCH. The running stitch is a very short, even stitch used for fine seaming, mending, gathering and other delicate sewing. The running stitch is usually a permanent stitch when used for sewing projects or mending. Working from right to left, weave the point of the needle in and out of the fabric several times before pulling the thread through. Keep the stitches and spaces between them small and even.

If the thread twists or knots as you sew, let the thread dangle with the needle end down. Carefully slide your fingers down the thread and you will feel it untwist.

3 BACKSTITCH

When you get to the end of the sewing line, practice a BACKSTITCH, which will secure the thread so it won't pull loose, as shown in the next picture.

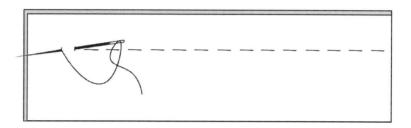

The BACKSTITCH is one of the strongest and most versatile of the hand stitches. It serves to secure hand stitching (at the beginning of the sewing line and at the end) and is the go-to stitch for repairing seams.

At the beginning and at the end of the hand stitching line, bring the needle and thread to the underside. Insert the needle through all fabric layers a stitch length **behind** and bring it up just in **back** of the point where the thread emerges. Pull the thread through. You can do this a couple of times to be certain the stitching is secure.

4 DUST CLOTH

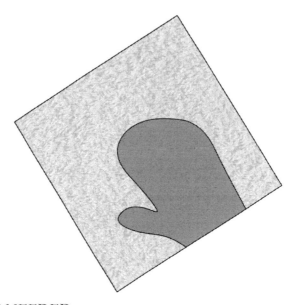

MATERIALS NEEDED:

Terry cloth or flannel fabric scraps
Gingham or cotton polyester fabric scrap
Thread to match

Cut a 12" x 12" piece of flannel or terry cloth fabric, using a pinking shears so no hemming is required. From the gingham or cotton polyester fabric cut a large hand shape (draw around your hand if you're the one doing the dusting). Pin the hand shape on one side of the square, and using the running stitch, sew small stitches all around the hand, leaving the bottom open to put your hand in. Don't forget to use the Backstitch at the beginning and end of the stitching to lock the stitches in place so the "hand" doesn't start to come loose.

This dust cloth is perfect for dusting the corners or intricate carvings on furniture or pictures because you're able to use your fingertips while dusting without getting them dirty.

5 STUFFED TIE SNAKE

Don't throw away those no-longer-used men's neckties. Using the running stitch, sew the back side of the necktie so it is sewn shut to both ends. On the narrow end, fold over the point and pin in place, then hand stitch the pointed part closed. Insert polyester filling material to stuff the tie to make it into a "snake", stuffing from the wide end all the way to the narrow, closed part of the tie. When finished stuffing the snake, turn down the pointed end and hand stitch it closed. Then, for a finishing touch, at the wide (head) end, add felt eyes and tongue, stitching them in place (don't forget to use the backstitch to secure the stitches in place). This is a quick "new" toy for children, and is also something that the children can help stuff. AND, older children who are learning to do hand sewing will be able to make these themselves!

6 FISH BEAN BAG

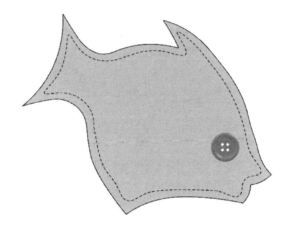

MATERIALS NEEDED

*Scraps of upholstery material, terry cloth, cotton fabric or felt

*Thread to match

*Buttons for eyes, or small circles of felt

*Polyester stuffing, or beans for a "real" bean bag

Fish bean bags are an easy hand sewing project for children, or for adults to make as toys for their children. Make several of them for kids to use for "bean bag toss", cornhole, or any number of bean bag games.

Pin the pattern piece (shown on following page) on doubled cloth (you'll need two pieces). Cut around the pattern adding a ¼" seam allowance all around.

Sew buttons in position for eyes on each piece, or glue small round pieces of felt for eyes. Pin the pattern pieces together, wrong side OUT, and using the running stitch, sew all around, leaving an opening in order to turn right side out. After sewing all around, turn right side out. Stuff with polyester stuffing or fill with beans. Stitch the opening closed.

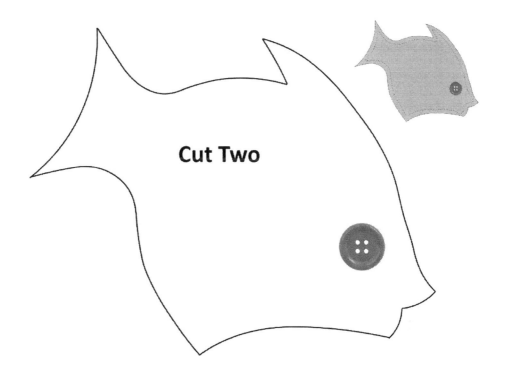

Cut Two

7 MARSHMALLOW PILLOW

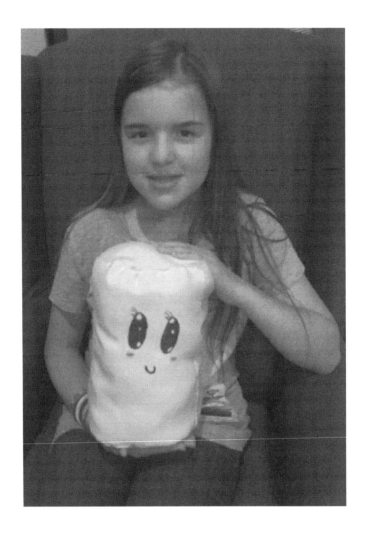

Marshmallow pillows are easy for kids to make and you can be sure they won't get lost because they won't leave the child's side!

MATERIALS NEEDED:

White fleece – 1/3 yard

Polyester fiberfill

Thread to match

1 Dessert plate (to make the top and bottom circle pieces)

Draw around the dessert plate on the fleece – you will need two of these circles for the top and bottom of the marshmallow.

Measure the distance around the plate (or measure the circle after it's drawn). Ours is 23".

Next, cut the "body" of the pillow – the measurement will be 23 ½" by 11" long (you need ONE of these).

With right sides together, pin the length portion (11") and using the running stitch, sew a ½" seam along the 11" length. You now have a cylinder shaped piece of fabric (marshmallow body).

With RIGHT sides together, pin the top circle of the marshmallow to the cylinder body. Hand sew a ½" seam to attach the top to the body.

Again, with RIGHT sides together, pin the bottom of the marshmallow to the cylinder body, leaving approximately 3" open (to stuff the marshmallow). Hand sew a ½" seam all around, leaving the 3" open area unsewn.

Turn the marshmallow right side out. Stuff marshmallow with polyester fiberfill, then pin the open area closed and hand stitch.

You can draw the face features with permanent markers, or fabric paint, glue on felt pieces or just leave the marshmallow pillow looking like a plain marshmallow.

8 OVERCAST STITCH

The next stitch you'll learn is the OVERCAST STITCH.

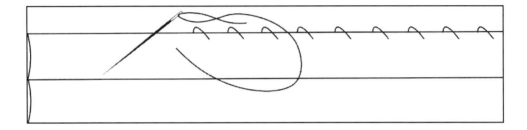

The OVERCAST STITCH is the usual hand stitch used for finishing raw edges of fabric to prevent them from raveling. The more the fabric ravels, the deeper and closer together the overcast stitches should be. The stitches can also be used as a decorative stitch on hand sewing items. Working from either direction, take diagonal stitches over the edge, spacing them an even distance apart at a uniform depth.

As previously suggested with the running stitch, we recommend you take a piece of scrap fabric and practice this stitch so you'll be comfortable with it when making your next project.

9 ELEPHANT BOOKMARK

Elephant bookmarks are easy and very inexpensive to make. Children and adults alike will appreciate the gift you've made for them.

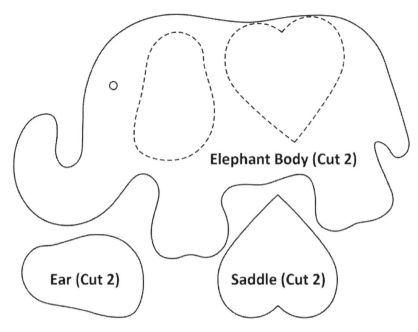

Elephant Body (Cut 2)

Ear (Cut 2)

Saddle (Cut 2)

Elephant Bookmark Pattern

MATERIALS NEEDED:

Scraps of two colors of felt

12-13 inch piece of ¾" grosgrain ribbon

Small bone or plastic ring

2 tiny beads for eyes

Small amount of polyester fiberfill

Crochet weight cotton thread to match

Cut out the felt pieces according to the chart above – two each of the elephant body, ears and saddle. Make the saddle pieces of a contrasting color.

Overcast around the ears and stitch to each side of the head, in the position shown in the sketch. Sew a bead on each side for the eyes. With overcast stitches, sew the two body sections together, stuffing as you go with the cotton batting.

Hinge the two heart-shaped saddle sections together at the top with a few stitches, then tack* to the top of the elephant back as a saddle. Pull the end of the ribbon through the center of the saddle and tack* underneath the saddle to the body.

Pull the top end of the ribbon through the ring, and fasten on the wrong side with a few stitches. Your finished elephant book mark will look like the illustration at the beginning of the pattern instructions.

**The term "tack" (tack to the top of the elephant back as a saddle) means to use just a few stitches to secure the saddle to the elephant back. Then after pulling the end of the ribbon through the center of the saddle, you will "tack" (secure the ribbon with a few…5 or 6…. stitches so it won't come loose) the ribbon underneath the saddle to the body

10 BUTTERFLY PINCUSHION

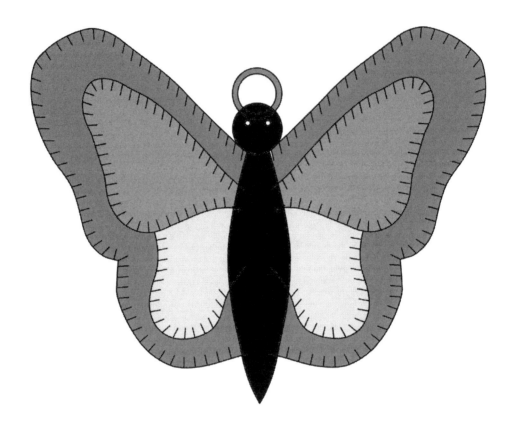

The butterfly pincushion takes very little time to make and you can just use scrap felt pieces, so I'd suggest making one for each of your "sewing" friends.

You will be using the Overcast Stitch on this project, so you'll be able to get a little extra practice using the stitch.

You can use any color felt scraps that you may have --- use any type of coordinating colors or contrasting colors that are handy. We've used green for the outer wings and yellow for the interior wings, and made solid green for the back. Use black embroidery floss to do the overcast stitch as indicated.

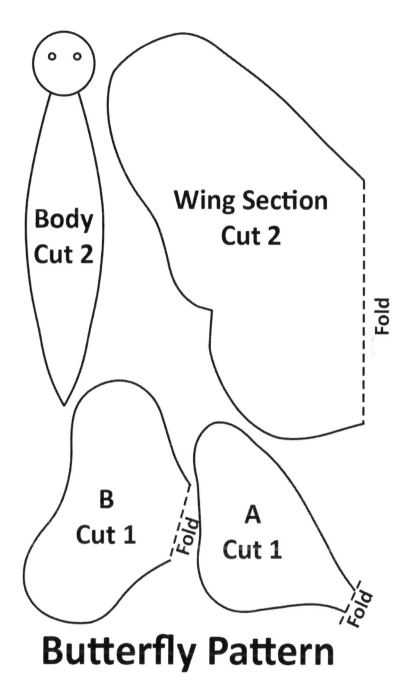

Butterfly Pattern

Using the pattern pieces above as a guide, cut the number of each piece as indicated - two of the large wing section on the fold (one for the front and one for the back). Cut two body sections, then cut one each of A and B on the fold, using contrasting colors if desired.

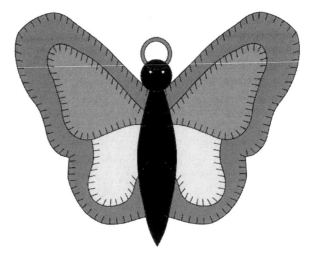

Pin wing sections A and B to the top of the large wing section as illustratcd, then using black embroidery floss stitch an overcast stitch all around wing sections A and B.

Next overcast the two body sections (front and back) together, using thread to match the body color or black as shown in the diagram, and lightly stuff with polyester fiberfill as you go. Before closing the opening at the head, make eyes with small stitches of yellow embroidery floss on the upper side.

Tack** the finished body to the upper wing section (front). Then overcast the front wing section to the back section, stuffing with polyester fiberfill as you go.

** The word "tack" means to sew small stitches along the body of the butterfly to secure it to the front wing section. This is done BEFORE you overcast the front finished wing section to the back wing section.

When finished, you can attach a small plastic ring behind the head for hanging, as shown above, or you can leave it as it is so it can lay on the sewing table.

11 FRENCH KNOT

The next project will use the Overcast Stitch as well as teaching you a new stitch, the FRENCH KNOT.

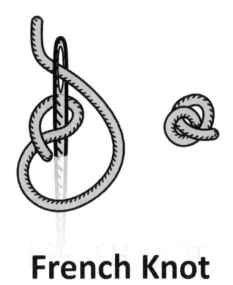

French Knot

The FRENCH KNOT is actually an embroidery stitch that has many applications for decorative stitching on clothing or craft items. Bring the needle up through the material, wrap the thread around the tip of the needle three to five times (depending on how big a knot you want) then insert the needle back into the fabric one or two threads away from where it was brought up. Draw the thread through carefully to form the knot on the right side. Bring the needle back up in position for the next "knot". They "knot" to the right in the drawing above demonstrates how the finished knot will look.

With some embroidery floss, take a scrap of fabric and practice making a few French Knots before starting on the next project.

12 HEART BOOKMARK

To make the Heart Bookmark you will be using the Overcast Stitch and French Knots to decorate the heart (we are also putting 28 small white beads in the materials needed list in case someone a little young or impatient wants to use them instead of making French Knots for decoration).

MATERIALS NEEDED:

2" Square of red felt

Strip of black felt 1 ½" x 12"

28 small white beads

1 red button – size of a nickel

Red embroidery floss

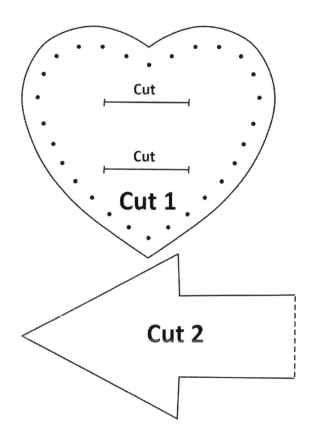

Using the pattern above, cut the heart from the red felt square. Cut along the two "cut" lines as indicated. Sew the white beads around the edge of the heart, or try your skill with French Knots (as described before this project) in place of the beads.

From the black felt, cut 2 strips 12 inches long, shaping one end like an arrow, following the outline above. Place one on top of the other and with red embroidery floss overcast the edges around the arrow shaped end, and about one-half inch on the arrow shaft. Slip one piece of the black felt strip through the heart, then matching the 2 strips, continue overcasting the edges of both pieces of felt to the end. Sew the button at the opposite end.

These bookmarks are so easily made that you can give one to each of your friends that love to read.

13 BLANKET STITCH

The next project will be made using a BLANKET STITCH.

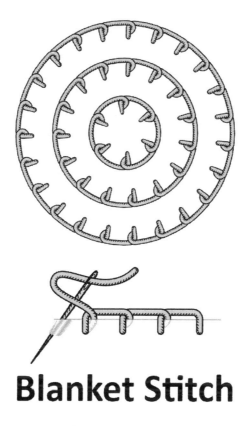

Blanket Stitch

The BLANKET STITCH, traditionally an embroidery stitch, can be used to cover fabric edges decoratively. Work from left to right, with the point of the needle and the edge of the work toward you. The edge of the fabric can be folded under or left raw. Secure the thread and bring out below the edge. For the first and each succeeding stitch, insert the needle through the fabric from right side and bring out at the edge. Keeping the thread from the previous stitch **under** the point of the needle, draw the needle and thread through, forming the stitch over the edge. Stitch size and spacing should remain the same.

As with the previous new stitches, we recommend you practice this Blanket Stitch on a small piece of felt or other scraps, so you'll be comfortable with the stitch as you start the next project.

14 COIN PURSE

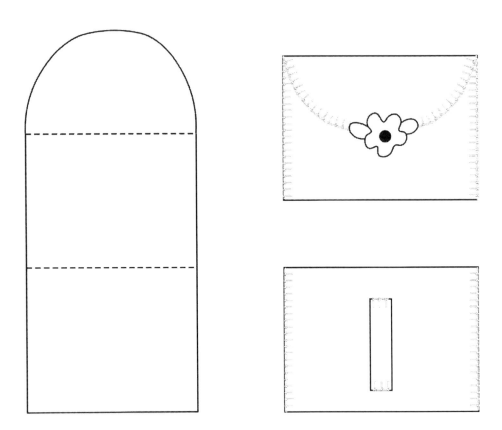

A coin purse is a very easy hand sewing project and something that would be useful for yourself, or to give as a gift.

Materials Needed:

1 10 x 12 or 9 x 12 piece of felt (your choice of color)

Felt scraps for trim

Coordinating color of yarn

1 snap

Cut a pattern for the coin purse like the diagram shown on the previous page. If you'd like the coin purse to be a little bigger or smaller, you can use a photocopy machine to make the pattern larger or smaller. Pin the pattern to the felt and cut out the purse. Fold the felt along the dotted lines as shown.

With the yarn, blanket stitch the sides together, being sure to take close, even stitches so it will hold together well. Next use the blanket stitch around the flap.

Sew the snap in place on the underside of the flap and to the purse. Cut a small flower and leaves or other design from the scraps of felt and carefully stitch them in place on top of the snap.

If you'd like, you can stitch a small strip of felt to the back of the purse as shown, to form a handle or so you can wear it on a belt.

15 DENIM POCKET KEY RING

MATERIALS NEEDED:

Denim Scraps

Metal Key Ring

Thread to match

Cut two pieces of denim 3 ¾ inches square. Cut the lower corners of the square so that the lower edge forms a triangular edge. Taper the sides slightly in at the top as shown in the drawing. Top stitch one piece, using small Running Stitches, so that it resembles a pocket. Fold the edges of both pieces under ¾" and press the seams.

Place pieces together, with wrong sides together. Topstitch with small Running Stitches, or Blanket Stitch the sides and bottom, leaving the top open. Cut a tab 2" long. Hem sides with small Running Stitches then fold around a metal key ring and insert in the top of the pocket. Sew the top shut.

16 BUTTERFLY APPLIQUE

Our easy to make butterfly appliqué can be used as a decoration all the way around the lower edge of an apron, as pictured above, or used individually on a pocket, purse, legs of your jeans, or make several on a fabric background to frame and hang on the wall.

Using the following pattern pieces, cut out the butterfly, using coordinating colors. Pin the pieces together following the diagrams above. Using the BLANKET STITCH sew the body of the butterfly to the wing sections, then using the same Blanket Stitch, attach the appliqué to the garment or craft item you wish to use it on.

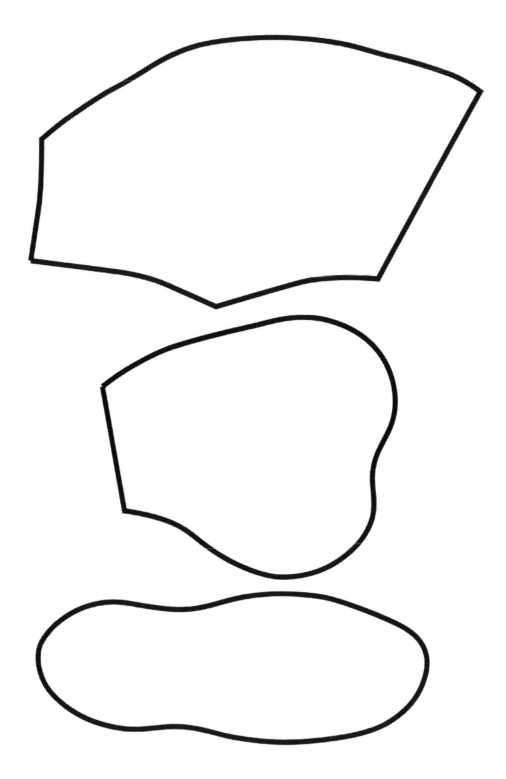

17 BABY BLOCKS

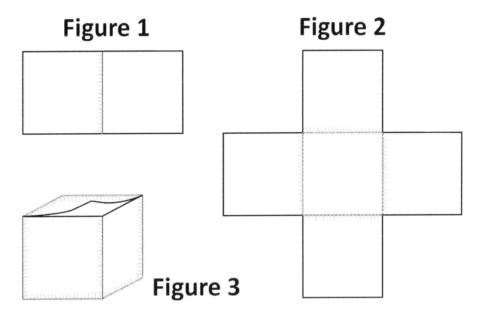

Figure 1   **Figure 2**

Figure 3

Soft, fabric washable baby blocks have no sharp corners to hurt the baby and can be used in many ways. You can use cotton duck fabric, or upholstery fabric or "oil" cloth, which is similar to what table cloths are made out of.

MATERIALS NEEDED:

¼ Yd each of 6 colors of fabric

1 Skein variegated yarn

Poly fiberfill stuffing

Using a yardstick, measure the fabric pieces into 3" strips and cut the strips. Next divide the strips into 3" squares, and cut. (Since each block takes only 6 squares, you'll have enough blocks to make several "sets" of blocks.

(1) Using the BLANKET STITCH, stitch two of the blocks together, making the stitches close together.

(2) Use one of the sewn squares as a "center" square or bottom of the block, then stitch three more squares on the other sides to form a cross.

(3) Bring each of the "sides" up and stitch the edges to form the outside of the block. The last fabric square will be attached at the top to complete the block. Stitch along two sides, leaving two seams open in order to stuff the block. Stuff the block firmly with the poly fiberfill then stitch the other two sides closed, and fasten the yarn securely so it will not come unstitched.

The blocks could be made with embroidered designs on some squares and numbers on other squares. In addition, a complete set of "alphabet" blocks could be made. A "set" of blocks could be six to the set, or ten or twelve, or as mentioned previously, a complete set of 26 blocks for the alphabet.

18 HEMMING STITCHES

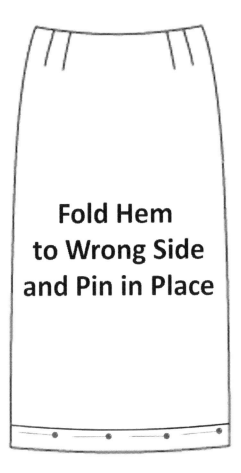

There are a few different stitches that can be used for hemming skirts, dresses and slacks, and we will cover three of them here. Be sure the garment is turned inside out, then fold the hem the desired length and pin in place. Try your hand with each of the following hemming stitches on scrap fabric before you start working on your garment.

19 SLANT HEMMING STITCH

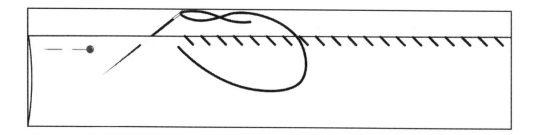

To work the SLANT HEMMING STITCH fasten the thread on the wrong side of the hem (the knot is on the wrong side of the hem), bringing the needle and thread through the hem edge. Working from right to left, take the first and each succeeding stitch approximately ¼" to 3/8" to the left, catching only one yarn of the garment fabric and bringing the needle down through the edge of the hem.

The SLANT HEMMING STITCH is the quickest to use and get done with the project, however it is the least durable because so much thread is exposed and subject to abrasion. (I would suggest you NOT use this stitch on slacks, as the constant pulling on and off, and possibly catching on a toe nail might pull the stitches loose).

20 SLIPSTITCH HEMMING STITCH

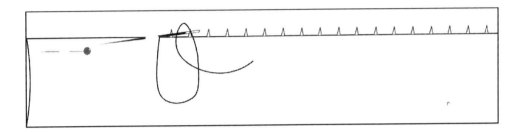

The SLIPSTITCH HEMMING STITCH is worked from right to left. Fasten the thread (knot) under the fold of the hem, then bring the needle and thread out through the fold of the hem. On the opposite side, in the **garment**, take a small stitch, catching only a few threads. Then, opposite from that stitch, in the **hem** edge, insert the needle and slip the needle through the fold for about ¼". Continue alternating the stitches in the same way to the end.

The SLIPSTITCH HEMMING STITCH is a durable and almost invisible stitch that would be very good to use on slacks, because the stitches are slipped through the fold of the hem edge, reducing the possibility of the thread catching and breaking.

21 VERTICAL HEMMING STITCH

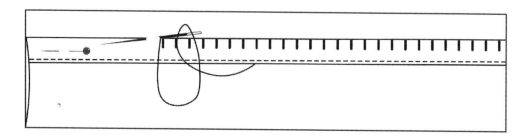

The VERTICAL HEMMING STITCH is a durable and stable stitch that is best suited for hems whose edges are finished with seam tape. The stitches are worked from right to left. Fasten the thread (knot) from the wrong side of the hem and bring the needle and thread through the hem edge. Directly **opposite** this point and beside the hem edge, begin the first and each succeeding stitch by catching only one thread of the garment fabric. Next direct the needle down diagonally to go through the hem edge approximately ¼" to 3/8" to the left. Short, vertical stitches will show on the hem.

22 BLIND HEM STITCH

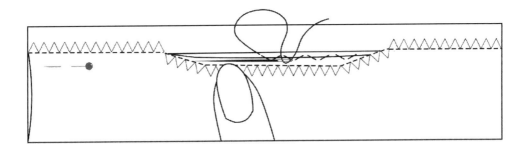

BLIND HEM STITCHES are made **inside**, between the hem and the garment (in this case between the two seam allowances that have been folded to the inside). Working from right to left with the needle pointing left, fold back the hem edge (you'll start at the right side of the heating pad). Start the needle so the thread knot is on the inside of the seams. Take a very small stitch on one side of the seam, then take a small stitch on the other side of the seam. Continue to alternate the stitches from one seam line to the other (or from garment to hem if you're working on a piece of clothing). Keep the stitches small and on the inside of the heating pad seam allowances, weaving the needle back and forth from seam to seam.

The following project will use the Blind Hem Stitch, so I would recommend that you practice a little with this hem before working on the next project.

23 MAKE YOUR OWN REUSABLE HEATING PAD

The reusable heating pad will use the running stitch that you've already used in several projects, plus we'll be using the new stitch – the Blind Hem Stitch.

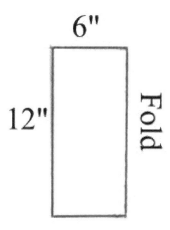

MATERIALS NEEDED:

12" X 12" piece of fleece – your choice of color

Matching thread

2 pound bag of rice

Fold the piece of fleece in half, right side to the inside. Pin in place. With the running stitch, using small stitches, sew one short side and the long side, using ¼" seams. Turn inside out. Fill with the rice. Fold the edges of the unsewn portion to the inside, using ¼" seam, pin the seam line. You'll use the following Blind Hem Stitch to close the heating pad:

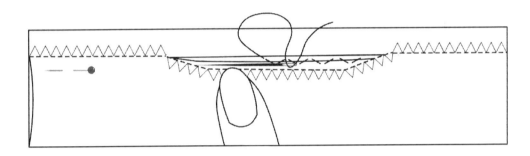

BLIND HEM STITCHES are made **inside**, between the hem and the garment (in this case between the two seam allowances that have been folded to the inside). Working from right to left with the needle pointing left, fold back the hem edge (you'll start at the right side of the heating pad). Start the needle so the thread knot is on the inside of the seams. Take a very small stitch on one side of the seam, then take a small stitch on the other side of the seam. Continue to alternate the stitches from one seam line to the other (or from garment to hem if you're working on a piece of clothing). Keep the stitches small and on the inside of the heating pad seam allowances, weaving the needle back and forth from seam to seam.

This rice filled heating pad can be put in the microwave for 1 minute for just the right amount of heat. My granddaughter, who made the **Narwhal Stuffed Toy Pattern** is the one who insisted on making this pattern and heating pad for her mother who has a sprained ankle. Way to go, young lady!!!

24 HOW TO DARN A HOLE IN A SOCK

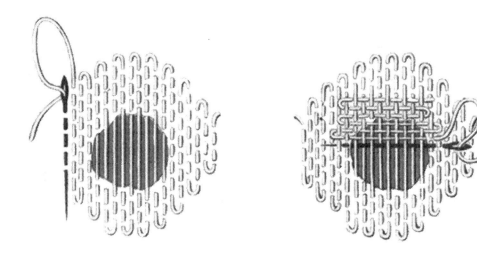

Parallel Running Stitches

So, you've gotten a hole in one of your favorite pairs of socks (or favorite sweater, or gloves). Don't throw them away – it is very easy to darn the hole and you'll never know where the hole was! This project uses the simple running stitch that you've used on several projects already, so this will be a breeze. Follow the easy steps provided and you'll have what looks like a new sock!

CHOOSE THE RIGHT COLOR OF THREAD.

If you'd like to hide the hole that you're darning you'll need to pick a thread that is close to the color of the existing sock yarn. If it doesn't match perfectly, that won't be a problem because you'll probably be the only one that ever sees your socks. Sweaters often come with extra "repair" thread that will match perfectly in hiding any holes or you can choose to use an alternate or complementary color for a whimsical look.

THREADING THE NEEDLE. Thread the needle with a length of thread approximately 20" long. Put the thread ends together and make a knot.

PUT SOMETHING STURDY INSIDE THE SOCK so you'll be able to see the hole easily. You can use a tennis ball or even a small pill container. Be sure the item isn't so big that it stretches the hole.

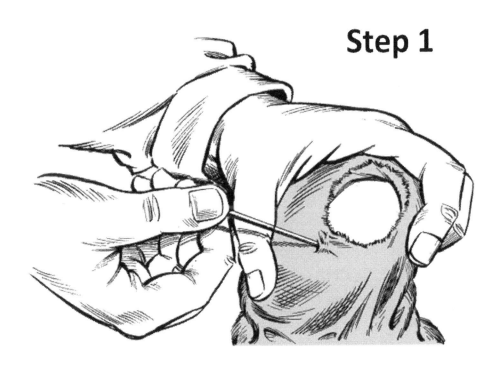

PUSH THE NEEDLE THROUGH ONE END OF THE HOLE. You will begin by sewing from the outside of the sock to the inside so that your knot is on the outside of the sock. (If it's on the inside it might rub against your feet and cause some irritation).

Step 2

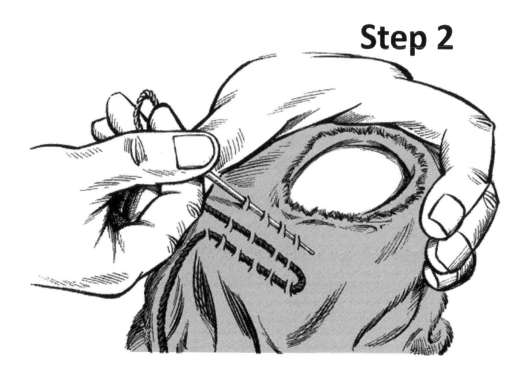

You are now going to make a large running stitch to the other side of the hole, running your needle and thread outside of the sock and in. Next make a stitch to the left and pull the needle back up and out of the sock again. Repeat your stitches. You will want to run your stitches in and over the hole, going back and forth until the hole is blocked up with parallel stitches, as shown in the following picture:

Step 3

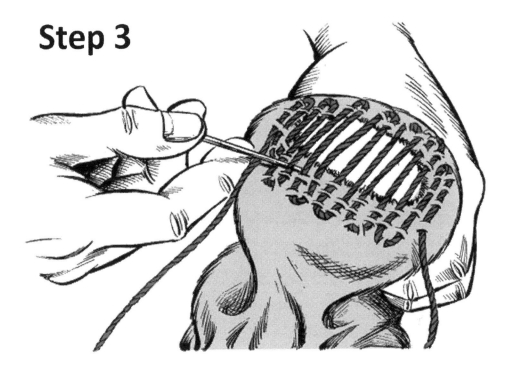

Finally, sew stitches perpendicular to the parallel stitches. You can weave your stitches in and out of the previous stitches in order to reinforce the patch you have created out of thread. When you are finished covering the hole, take a few very small stitches at the end to lock the stitches so they won't come loose.

25 CROSS STITCH

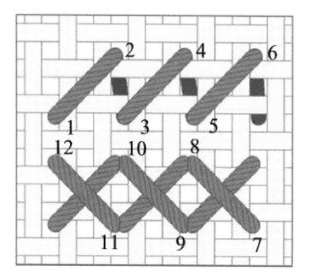

The CROSS STITCH of course is used in hundreds of cross stitch designs and wall hangings, but it can also be used as a decoration on sleeves or hems of skirts, on accessories and more. Use your imagination and put the Cross Stitch to good use!

Working from left to right, starting at the #1 position, push the needle up from underneath (the knot in the thread will be on the underside). The first stitch is a slanted stitch to #2. Run the needle through #2 and down vertically (thread underneath the fabric) to #3, then horizontally to #4, then down vertically (thread underneath the fabric) to #5, then horizontally to #6.

In this small pattern, your next vertical stitch will be down to #7 (thread on the underside of the fabric). You are now ready to work the stitches back to the beginning to finish the "X's". First, do a parallel stitch to #8, vertical stitch to #9 (thread underneath the fabric), parallel to #10, vertical to #11, and parallel to #12, completing the cross stitch pattern. Be sure to make a knot on the underside of #12 before cutting the thread so the stitches won't pull out.

26 E-Z SEW SEWING CARDS

Teach Your Child To Sew With E-Z Sew Sewing Cards! E-Z Sew sewing cards teach the young child (ages 3-7) how to sew, in addition to teaching dexterity and eye-hand coordination. E-Z Sew sewing cards provide a sense of accomplishment as your child "sews" the object giving you more time for your own sewing projects.

Each of the following sewing cards can be printed on white cardstock. Cut out the objects then using a round hole punch, punch out the small black spots around the objects. These holes will be where the child "sews", weaving a shoestring back and forth all around the object.

You can use colored yarn (about a 20" – 24" length) as the "thread" for the child to sew with. Or, as mentioned above, a shoestring makes a great "thread" because of the "tip" that may make the sewing a bit easier.

We will include four different sewing card objects you can print and have ready for your youngster. For a bigger selection of sewing cards, please refer to **E-Z Sewing Cards** at **SewWithSarah.com**.

27 THREAD HANGER

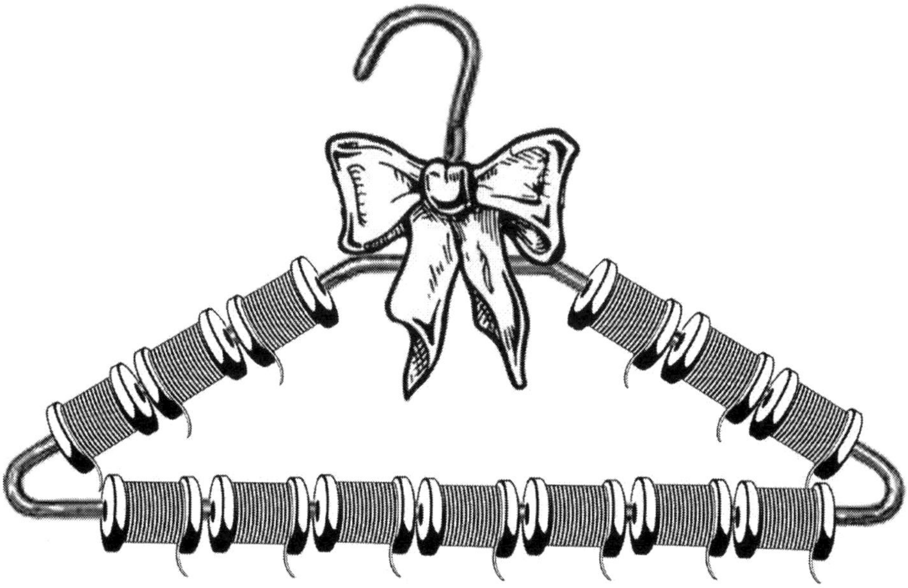

Thread Hanger - Super simple, but VERY popular with everyone that sews!!

One of the handiest gifts you could give to the sewer or crafter is our "thread hanger". It can be hung on the back of a chair within easy reach for hand work, or can be taken along in a car so you can do your hand work while riding and not have to "chase" your spools of thread around the car.

Begin with an ordinary coat hanger and loosen the top with pliers and straighten it out. Wrap the wire with ribbon, catching the ribbon at the ends with a few stitches, or just leave the hanger as it is. String many spools of thread on the wire, using an assortment of colors, and put it back in shape. Decorate the handle with ribbons or a big bow. At the end of the ribbons tie small strawberry or heart shaped pin cushions. When thread is needed it can be pulled from the spool easily without removing the spool from the thread hanger.

28 RESOURCES

PATTERN PAPER

Pattern paper is probably the most used sewing notion that sewers and crafters have. Pattern paper is used for making patterns, altering patterns, drawing out possible designs to make, plus much more. The most practical type of pattern paper would be the type that could be re-used without tearing and can be pinned to fabric without tearing. The pattern paper we recommend is "Pellon's Easy Pattern 830" pattern paper.

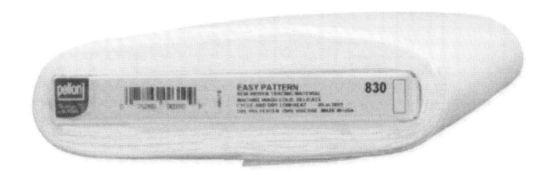

Pellon's Easy Pattern 830 pattern paper is 45" wide and comes in 10 yard bolts, which I've found to be just the right amount for my current projects and have handy for additional projects.

I use Easy Pattern 830 for every pattern I make, as well as for making craft patterns, and doing alterations on clothing items. I have some patterns that were made over 15 years ago, and I can bring them out, press the pattern paper pieces, and they're ready for me to use again.

http://SewWithSarah.com ~ Your sewing, craft, pattern and pattern making headquarters for over 40 years! Items available are online pattern making classes, downloadable sewing patterns for men, women and children, sewing repair books, craft books and patterns plus much more!

http://PatternsThatFitYou.com ~ The online fashion design school teaches the art of custom fitting patterns and pattern making to beginners and experts alike.

http://Patterns2Go.com ~ A variety of patterns to choose from – sewing, crafting, knitting, crochet, tatting, and more.

http://SewMachineRepair.com ~ Learn how to repair your own treadle, serger and sewing machines and save yourself time, money and frustration.

http://101WaysToTieAScarf.com ~ Scarves, the versatile accessory! Learn how to make scarves and 101 ways to tie them.

http://SewWithLeather.com ~ Everything you need to know about sewing with leather.

http://SewingBusiness.com ~ Information plus tutorials for those who sew and for those in the business of sewing for others.

ABOUT THE AUTHOR

Sarah Doyle learned to sew at the age of 8 on her mother's treadle Sewing machine, and found a lifelong passion.

Sarah officially started her sewing and pattern making career in 1970 with a military assignment to Taiwan. She had been taking in sewing and alterations to help make ends meet for their family of 6 children, when her husband received orders for Taiwan. She was excited about the prospect of being able to learn something about Oriental pattern making because it would give her a chance to "make patterns that would fit my customers perfectly".

Sarah attended a yearlong pattern making class at a local Taiwanese school with the help of an English speaking Taiwanese lady, then she began writing her first book, "Sarah's Key To Pattern Drafting".

After returning to the U.S., Sarah started teaching pattern drafting classes to the general public as well as "for credit" classes for home economics teachers. She then made the classes available by mail order so those who could not attend her classes would also have the opportunity to learn pattern making.

With the internet explosion, a fast paced society, and so little time for organized classes, Sarah once again filled a real need for the sewers around the world by painstakingly setting up and making available online every class, book and pattern she had authored.

Starting with just one book "Sarah's Key to Pattern Drafting" and a long list of people wanting that book in 1976, Sarah now has over 35 sewing, pattern making, pattern make-over, craft, quilting, embroidery, sewing machine repair and general how-to books available, in addition to a line of clothing patterns for plus size children.

Made in United States
Orlando, FL
01 November 2023

38485533R00033